THE
FORD CAPRI
STORY

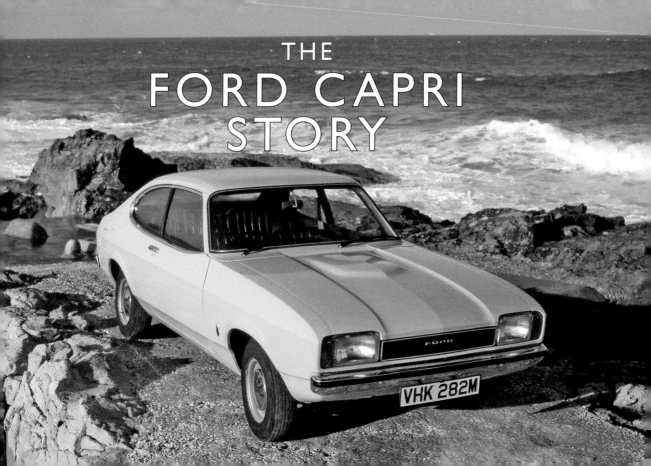

THE FORD CAPRI STORY

Giles Chapman

The
History
Press

BHK 532Y

Published in the United Kingdom in 2012 by
The History Press
The Mill · Brimscombe Port · Stroud · Gloucestershire · GL5 2QG

British Library Cataloguing in Publication Data
A catalogue record for this book is available from the British
Library.

Hardback ISBN 978-0-7524-8461-7

Typesetting and origination by The History Press
Printed in Great Britain

It's hard, today, to appreciate just how limited the choices were if you wanted motoring excitement in the mid-1960s.

Supercars for playboys and pools winners aside, there was no dearth of sports cars on offer from the likes of MG, Fiat and Triumph and, on a somewhat more rarefied and stylish level, Alfa Romeo, Jaguar, Lancia, Lotus and Porsche. High performance with a metal roof was on attainable offer from the Mini Cooper, BMW 2002, Triumph Vitesse and sundry others. Quite a line-up. And that was even before you counted specialist and kit cars from Morgan and TVR, or esoteric imports like the NSU 1200TT or Renault 8 Gordini. So what was the issue?

Well, all of them had significant drawbacks for the driver on a fairly limited budget and intending to use the car on a daily basis.

The high cost alone put a quality Porsche or BMW well out of reach for most. Ditto Alfas, Jaguars, Lancias and Lotuses, only all those were temperamental or complex and expensive to run into the bargain. The Vitesse, though fast, was a bag of nails; a Morgan offered a very narrow appeal – fun but eccentric. The Mini Cooper was tiny and basic and the sports cars were, well, sports cars, with the traditions of a cramped cockpit, harsh ride and a hood likely to admit draughts and moisture on most days of the year just about anywhere in mid-northern Europe.

Somehow, indefinably, there was a gap in the market for something with all or most of the best sports car attributes and few if not none of the drawbacks. A car that was cheap to buy and run, fun to drive, and – very important, this – got you admiring

glances. There was a dormant stratum of consumers, passionate about cars but not the sort of upper-crust anoraks to be found reading *Motor Sport* magazine, waiting to be awoken.

And one company decided to give the public exactly what it fancied. The Ford Capri phenomenon was about to be unleashed on an unsuspecting world. Here's how it happened.

◀ The Capri, an eternally handsome car, is seen here in its very final form, as the limited-edition 280 in Brooklands green paint.

ooks about Ford and its dozens of great car designs over more than 110 years have a tendency to begin with Henry Ford, the Model T, the birth of mass production and the worn-smooth quote 'Any colour, as long as it's black'. For the purposes of this book on quite possibly the best-loved model Ford's European arm has ever

◄ Until this Anglia 105E came along in 1959, with its rev-happy engine and four-speed gearbox, Britain's economy cars had been a chore to drive.

devised, we leapfrog all that and find ourselves in Essex in the early 1960s, where the Ford Motor Company is thriving like no other car manufacturer in Britain.

You can pinpoint the moment when the fortunes – and the image – of the company really started to outpace competitors like British Motor Corporation (Austin, Morris), Rootes Group (Hillman, Humber) and General Motors (Vauxhall) to the day in October 1959 when the Ford Anglia 105E was unveiled. The moment, really, had little to do with its natty, sharp-angled design – in fact *that* was disliked by many, who deemed the American-style reverse-sloped rear window awkward and gimmicky. What the Anglia had was responsiveness. Its 997cc engine was the very latest in overhead-valve design, and it actually seemed to enjoy being revved. Not only that but the Anglia was the first British small car with a four-speed gearbox that could take the strain out of driving on Britain's newly launched motorway network. Apart from the brand new and highly unconventional Mini, the Anglia was the only other British small car that was genuinely enjoyable to drive.

The Anglia proved extremely popular, becoming the first Ford in Britain to reach one million sales. It also paved the way for the Ford Cortina, a simple family car so in tune with the needs of the average British motorist that it would top the country's sales chart for 10 of the 20 years it was in Ford showrooms. After that, and with the previously isolated British and German subsidiaries of Ford now working together in the newly-created Ford of Europe, the company pulled off the same trick in the van market, with the Transit. Along the way, there were also-rans, such as the Corsair, and a few total duds. Chief among those were the Consul Classic and Consul

With its flamboyant styling, including tail fins, the Consul Capri – cool though it now looks – was something of a 1950s throwback.

Probably the best photo ever of the Ford Corsair (which donated its V4 engine to the Capri): Corsair GT, Jim Clark, model Jean Shrimpton and, behind the camera, David Bailey.

Capri of 1961 – a pair of leaden performers with heavy structures and fussy styling that seemed to take the worst of late 1950s Detroit fins-and-chrome and scale it down to fit a European car package.

The Consul Capri was not without a certain tacky appeal, because all the side windows could be wound down to turn it into a pillarless coupé for cruising the seafront at Southend, Filey or Weston-super-Mare. Today it does look pretty cool and, at the time, it was the sportiest car Ford in Britain had ever offered. The very limited production Capri GT could nudge 95mph too, but its dynamic roadholding shortcomings were all too evident on corners. By 1964 it had been axed anyway because the Ford Cortina saloon, in both GT and Lotus forms, was a far superior prospect for enthusiastic drivers.

Ford in the USA, meanwhile, had for some time been tackling the idea of a new type of car to boost its humdrum image. It recognised that it simply did not produce automobiles that appealed to young people or had a scintilla of sportiness to them. Even the Thunderbird was something of an old man's car, best suited to the newly retired Florida set. The catalyst for change was a brash young Italian-American business

▶ Ford's 1954 Thunderbird had a sporty feel at first, but soon came to represent sprightly American retirement rather than youthful energy.

▶▶ Lessons in style: an open-air debrief about Consul and Zephyr MkIIs in the late 1950s showed Ford of Britain's tightening focus on design.

18

hotshot called Lee Iacocca. You may be grateful to him today for starting the MPV era, when he instigated the first multi-passenger vehicle in a later post at Chrysler, but in 1962 he was a Ford vice-president.

That year, Ford designers and engineers presented him with the latest results of their efforts – a dagger-shaped two-seater sports-racer with a German Ford V4 engine mounted behind the driver and passenger. They'd called it Mustang, and it was so well developed that in October 1962 Stirling Moss put it through its paces for some demonstration laps before the open-mouthed crowds at the Watkins Glen race circuit.

Lee Iacocca, however, remained unmoved. His instincts cut in like a turbocharger.

'When I looked at the guys praising it,' he said, 'the offbeat crowd, the real buffs, I thought: "That's sure not the car we want to build because it can't be a volume car. It's too far out".'

You could have argued with Iacocca, then aged 37, but you'd have had trouble winning. He knew what customers would buy – his career at the company, after being recruited as a Princeton-fresh graduate, was built on making Philadelphia the number one territory in Ford's national American sales league.

So the original Mustang brief was shelved (although the car did influence the design of the Ford GT40 sports-racer) and Iacocca's new one created. His extraordinary grasp of unfolding demographics told him that the market was ripe for a car that was *sporty* rather than an actual sports car. Something desirable without being off-putting. The customers were of the post-war 'baby-boomer' generation, who were staying single (or, at least, childless) for longer as they pursued careers and burnt their way through that addictive new commodity: disposable income.

◄◄ A full-size 1962 styling exercise called Saxon gave an idea of how a two-seater sports version of the Cortina might work.

➤ The very first Mustang was this rear-engined two-seater, eventually deemed just too radical to put on public sale.

◀ Godfather of the Mustang, on the right, Lee Iacocca with his baby; the other car is Ford's best-selling 1960 Falcon, with Ford executive Don Frey.

They were more Mary Tyler Moore than Samantha from *Bewitched*. They didn't need, or really want, the traditional American sedan – even in its new so-called 'compact' size – but an imported two-seater roadster was just too risqué. What they craved was a 'personal' car. Something, well, just like the Mustang that Iacocca and Ford gave them.

Ford's design team, led by Gene Bordinat, created a starched-smart two-plus-two around the mechanical components of the Ford Falcon, retaining only the side air vents (now dummies) from the original Mustang concept. There was little fussy chrome ornamentation and the look was determinedly crisp and European.

Such was the hype surrounding the Mustang when it appeared at the New York World Fair on 17 April 1964 that the first cars were auctioned to the highest bidders: tales abounded of anxious buyers sleeping in their cars overnight while the cheque cleared, to ensure they weren't gazumped. In that first model year, 1964, 418,000 were sold, and sales topped a million by 1966, making it the first vaguely sporty car ever to reach this dizzy sales pinnacle.

Did You Know?

The Capri MkI was surprisingly successful in the USA, making its debut at the 1970 New York motor show. It was retailed through Ford's upmarket Lincoln Mercury Division, and more than half a million were sold there, all of them built in Ford's Cologne plant. By contrast, the MkII was an utter failure in the States, with only small numbers sold in 1976 and '77, when so-called 'Federal' specification assembly was axed in August.

◄ The 1964 Mustang 'personal' car was a winner from the off for Ford, plugging into America's 'baby boomer' prosperity.

Sweetheart of
the Supermarket Set

It had to be. With non-stop thrift, with extra-nimble performance, with all-around, All-American elegance, Mustang has become the sweetheart of the Supermarket Set.

They like the way it makes sense with gas. More miles per gallon is about the heart of it. They relish the way Mustang maneuvers into tight parking spots, the good performance of the 200-cubic-inch Six on the open road.

And Mustang makes people feel just great. Great at the supermarket . . . grand at the opera . . . casually elegant everywhere. (Why not, with bucket seats, snappy stick shift, plush carpeting and all the other no-cost specials that a Mustang features?)

Why not make a date for a test-drive? You, too, can go places with the sweetheart of the Supermarket Set!

Between 1964 and 1966, the era of the original Mustang, 1,288,557 were shifted.

In the minds of car buffs, these early Mustangs are defined by the Shelby GT-350, a pioneering 'muscle car' created in 1965 by Texan Carroll Shelby and featuring high-powered V8 engines transplanted into modified Mustang carcases. But this is utterly misleading. The typical Mustang, though, was an automatic six-cylinder machine for cruising through the suburbs, probably a hardtop coupé and loaded with as many electric gadgets as the owner's hire purchase limits would allow. For Ford had also mastered the art of menu-pricing the Mustang: you could specify your car any which way. You could choose between three body styles – fastback coupé, convertible and hardtop coupé – and then add any one of five engine options, from a puny 101bhp straight six to a fiery 271bhp V8. Then there were six transmission options, three

This 1965 Mustang ad shows where the sporty car was pitched: at the upwardly-mobile heart of American suburbia.

The GT40, shown here in the 24-hour Le Mans endurance race in 1965 driven by Innes Ireland and John Whitmore, massively perked up Ford's public image.

suspension packages, three braking set-ups, three wheel sizes and dozens of style and comfort choices. It all helped reinforce Ford's claim that here was the first ever 'personal car'. Outsiders nicknamed it the 'pony car', a term which soon came to refer to any kind of mass-produced sporty coupé that could be had with engines ranging from feeble to fearsome.

The Mustang seemed as exotic and glamorous as anything from Italy when the first few found their way to the UK in 1964/65. A white Mustang convertible – never mind what engine – was a total film star machine, ideal for photo-ops outside Pinewood or burbling lazily through Antibes. Ford never offered it with right-hand-drive, and that just added to the mystique of glimpsing one here.

The entire Mustang phenomenon, hugely enhanced by the fact that it could justly be called the fastest-selling car in history, set Ford of Europe thinking. Could the success, perhaps, be replicated in the Old World?

In 1964, the venture was unofficially kick-started, as initial design sketches and concepts began to be generated in studios both in the USA and the UK. A full-size mock-up of the Saxon was lurking in the Essex design studio, a potential two-seater coupé based on the Cortina and created in 1962 by resident Ford stylist John Fallis, while Stirling Moss had had a Cortina modified into a fastback coupé by

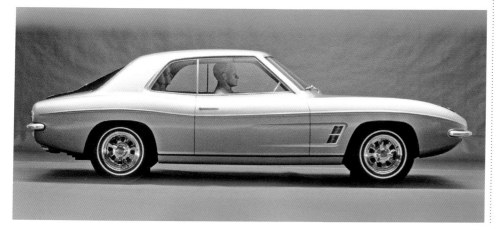

◄ Early ideas for the Capri's shape were actually quite bland; note the fake air intakes ahead of, rather than behind, the doors.

➤ Not quite in Capri territory but this four-seater fastback Cortina was still Stirling Moss's daily driver for a time. It was custom-built by Ogle Design.

➤➤ A sketch of one Capri design proposal adopted the 'Coke bottle' wing-line with a pillar-less coupé upper section.

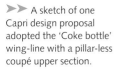

Ogle Design for his personal use. So there was plenty of two-and three- dimensional food for thought to get the creative juices flowing.

There was also 29-year-old Ford stylist Phil Clark, newly arrived in February 1964 from the USA where he'd been closely involved in the whole Mustang project

➤ A step on from the previous image, this normalised side elevation is very American in feel, actually resembling later Chrysler cars.

➤ This undeniably dramatic design hints at the Capri's eventual side window shape; the rest of it is pretty fanciful.

There's a lot of the mid-/late 1960s Mustang to this Capri rendering, yet the Capri's outline and hardpoints are beginning to coalesce.

since the start – indeed, he even created the world-famous galloping horse Mustang logo. He would be the chief exterior stylist for the new car, heading a team of designers from the UK and Germany.

Right from the off, product planners and designers agreed the car needed to be a four-seater, and the design direction began to coalesce under the codename GBX. Early work shows a clear American influence in renderings of a typical 'mid-Atlantic' hardtop coupé with an undulating waistline – the so-called 'Coke bottle' profile – but throughout 1965 and '66 the shape evolved and began to gather its own distinctive touches. Under Phil Clark's close guidance, the long bonnet/short boot look emerged, the near-fastback rear window

The design of the car comes together in this close-to-finished Project Colt styling model towards the end of 1966.

was added to the abruptly truncated tail, and the hockey stick-shaped crease in the side panels appeared. Just like the Mustang, and harking back to that funny prototype of 1962 and the GT40 Le Mans car, fake air intakes were added just behind the two doors to give the vague impression that this was a mid-engined competition machine

▲ Ford staff monitor the flow of fluttering paper strips on the Colt as testing gets underway to refine its wind-cheating abilities.

whose powerful engine and manful brakes needed to be kept as cool as the dude at the wheel.

Stylistically, the essence of the GBX shape was settled on in July 1966, after full-size mock-ups had gone down extremely well at customer clinics held that spring in London, Cologne and Milan. At this point Ford bosses in Europe and at the USA mothership were now so convinced the car was a potential winner that the countdown towards production began. GBX was officially renamed 'Project Colt', investing it with Mustang-like expectations for winning

◀ Ford's white-coated modelling team gather to turn a huge lump of clay into the Capri's final shape.

the sales derby. Some £20m was allocated to developing it in secret, with much of that budget (Ford ended up splashing £22m) going on re-tooling factories in Cologne, Germany, and Halewood on Merseyside in the UK to manufacture the car.

➤ It looks messy but, in an age before computer-aided design, this was the only way to get a car's form spot-on.

➤➤ Here two members of staff are taking mouldings from their handiwork at Ford's secret design studio complex.

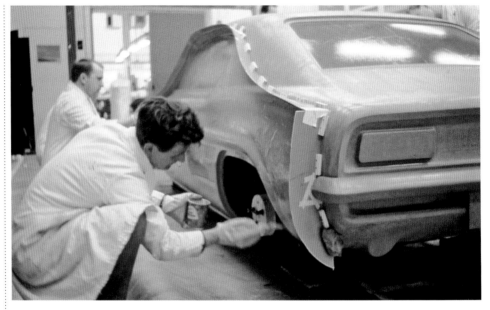

Engineers, led by the hugely experienced John Hitchman, were soon carrying out exhaustive testing of running prototypes but, in doing so, something crucial emerged about the car's shape. People travelling in the back seats during these tests found, to a man, that the experience was an imprisoning, claustrophobic one, with the massive rear roof pillars making a view out well nigh impossible. Phil Clark's body

design team was forced to come up with a solution in short order, and they found it in a styling trick used for years by Jaguar, that of an elegantly tapering, U-shaped rear quarter window that opened up the rear passenger compartment without ruining the overall sleekness of the car.

And nor was that the last fundamental change required before launch. 'Colt' was all set to be the car's actual title until it was discovered it had been registered globally by Japan's then obscure Mitsubishi Motors. The same thinking caps that had come up with 'Cortina' now revisited the map of Europe and alighted on the sun-kissed island resort in the Bay of Naples. Fortunately, that name had also been in use by Ford's Lincoln division in the US since 1952. So Capri it would be . . . usually resolutely mispronounced, with the emphasis on the second syllable rather than the first. Yet to a rain-soaked, seemingly cash-strapped Britain, then just beginning to expect foreign holidays in the sun reached via jet plane, it spoke eloquently of the high life so perfectly epitomised by the opening sequence of *The Italian Job*.

◄ Here, a clay modeller is giving shape to the steering column binnacle and other aspects of the dashboard.

Capris started to be produced in Germany and at Ford's Halewood plant in November 1968. Here, it shared the Merseyside production line with the recently introduced Ford Escort (the last Ford car to be entirely designed in Britain). And there was good sense in it doing so, because much of the unseen metal hardware under the Capri's attractive lines was shared with the Escort.

Following a media briefing in Bonn, Germany, on 21 January 1969, the wraps came off the car, to gasps of delight from customers and gnashing of teeth from competitors, at the Brussels Motor Show three days later. The Capri arrived in Ford showrooms just two weeks later, but many commuters were also treated to their own preview of the car that was set to shake up the motoring world. On launch day, 5 February, Ford parked a gleaming new Capri outside every major railway station in the south-east of England. In the newspapers those bemused train travellers unfolded were the first advertisements in Ford's campaign for the car, under the intriguing slogan: 'The car you always promised yourself'.

▼ A real steering wheel is carefully used to get the relationship between the various interior elements just right.

The immaculate
Colt prototype, finally
completed in 1968
but still dogged by a
claustrophobic outlook for
rear seat passengers.

➤ Cold weather testing well underway for the Ford Colt, soon to emerge as the slightly redesigned, and retitled, Capri.

➤➤ As the Capri was being readied for the showroom, Ford's GT40 was still going great guns on-track, here about to clinch fourth in the 1968 Spa 1,000km race.

45

➤ The freshly-minted 1969 Ford Capri, seen here in 2000GT guise, was set to change the way people selected a sporty car.

➤➤ Semi-fastback styling concealed the fact that the new Capri was a four-seater; this is a German-market GXL.

Was this entirely true? Nothing quite like the Capri had been available before, so how could you have pledged one to the inner self as a reward for dutifully schlepping backwards and forwards to the office every day? *Car* magazine bashed the nail sardonically on the head when it said: 'It's the latest, the greatest, and just what you've always wanted – as long as you're Mr Average to the Ford market researchers.' For here was a sexy GT without the highly-strung engineering, four decent seats behind a long bonnet, and at prices little higher than ordinary saloons. The list of options was so extensive that it seemed every car would come with a unique specification.

This matrix system echoed the personalised approach that had made the Mustang such a hit. You selected your own Capri using a series of 'building blocks'. The starting point was the engine, and to begin with there was a choice of crossflow-head, straight-four cylinder 1.3 and 1.6 'Kent' or 2.0-litre V4 units. Then you could either accept the base, rather austere, trim level, or dress it up with an X pack (adding comfortable interior touches), an L pack (exterior embellishments) or an R pack (for a pseudo-rally, boy racer livery including a

We were going to call the new Capri a 2+2.
But there's too much room in the back.

We know some people will find it hard to be-
lieve that the Capri is a four seater.
It's understandable.
Most cars that look like the Capri are either
straightforward two seaters. Or two-plus-two's.
Which in most cases means a two seater with an
upholstered shelf in the back. That'll take a bag of
golf clubs.

Or somebody small who bends easily.
We've gone out of our way to ensure there's enough
room inside for adults to make themselves comfortable.
The five seats are deep, wide and sumptu-
ously sprung. The back seats you can sit back
and relax in. Without your legs going to
sleep. As it stands the Capri is a
pretty luxurious motor car.

But if you want to make changes you can. One of the Capri
Custom Plans includes reclining front seats and contoured
rear seats with a fold-away armrest.
Other plans offer other possibilities for personalising
your Capri. But one thing you can't do—
you can't turn it into a 3-seater.

Ford leads the way.

CAPRI Ford

▲ A very 'period' 1969 MkI GT with characteristic matt black bonnet and Rostyle wheels and, in this case, the most popular 1600 engine.

▲ The driver's seat does seem to be pushed as far forward as it will go, but it was reasonably comfy in the back for two.

48

matt-black bonnet). Your dealer could then talk you into a combination of some of them to create an XL or, for GTs only, XLR (but not an XR or LR). So many different types of Capri were available that no dealer could possibly stock all 26 of them. If truth be told, there were too many derivatives at first. This catalogue traffic-jam was systematically slimmed down in the years that followed.

Prices? That was the most amazing thing. The base 1300 sold for £890 – compare that to a decidedly unsexy Austin 1300GT at £909 – and the 2000GT for only £1,088 although seatbelts, either fixed or inertia reel, cost extra.

➤ This 1970 ad stresses the enormous number of choices available to custom-create your own version of the early car.

FACTS & DATA: CAPRI MKI 1300GT

Announced: 1969

Engine capacity, configuration: 1298cc, straight-four cylinder

Engine bore/stroke: 80.98/62.99mm

Engine power output: 64bhp @ 6000rpm

Fuel system: single carburettor

Bodystyle: two-door, four-seater coupé

Wheelbase: 2559mm

Length: 4262mm

Width: 1646mm

Height: 1275mm

Top speed: 93mph

Acceleration, 0–60mph: 14.8 seconds

Fuel consumption, average: 26mpg approx

Price when new: £986 (in 1969)

Did You Know?

The first of many special edition models was introduced in September 1971. It was based on the 1600GT or 2000GT, painted in bright vista orange, and came with black plastic rear window slats and a bootlid-mounted spoiler – a treatment copied from certain editions of the Ford Mustang.

➤ With a wide variety of well-proven Ford engines under its bonnet, owners were guaranteed low running costs.

The German-made line-up was largely similar, although the engine range was different in that it consisted entirely of locally-manufactured V4 engines in 1.3-, 1.5-. 1.7- and 2.0-litre sizes and, within a few weeks of launch, a supplementary 2.3-litre compact V6 variant was added too.

Ford in the UK went even further in September 1969 when it introduced some genuine, big-engined muscle into the range with the arrival of a 3-litre V6 'Essex' engine in the car, initially in GT livery only but joined in March 1970 by the 3000E, a tasty 'Executive' luxury model that looked the business with its vinyl roof, cloth-insert seats, chrome side strips and opening rear quarterlight windows.

▲ This original-style dashboard would only continue until 1972, when a long-lived update was announced.

◄ A sliding steel sunroof was one of the more expensive options; note how the black bonnet paint continues over the top halves of the doors.

▲ The Capri cut a completely new dash on Europe's streets – comparable style to an Italian GT with nothing highly-strung under the bonnet.

▲ Even in its plainest form – this is a European-market 1300XL – the Capri could still suggest a jet-set lifestyle, sort of.

The Germans added their own big V6 engine option but at a 2.6-litre size in the slick 2600GT. Ford's Cologne team then took this car and turned it into the RS2600, a limited-run special designed to qualify the Capri for European saloon car racing. Its 120mph performance was achieved by specifying Kugelfischer fuel injection for the engine, and by fitting four-wheel ventilated disc brakes, while bumpers were lightweight quarter sections and wheels were four-spoke alloys. The first 50 were pure racing cars, the rest roadgoing hot rods. Within a year of launch, the Capri family formed a pan-European range of cars that seemed anything but mass-produced.

◀ This striking Capri GT has the 1.7-litre V4 engine option exclusive to models built at Ford's German plant in Cologne.

Stylistically and technically, the Capri's nearest competitors at the time of its launch, and for some years afterwards, were probably the MGB GT and MGC GT, the rather old-fashioned fastback Sunbeam Rapier, and maybe even the then brand-new Reliant Scimitar GTE with its novel glassfibre bodyshell. They all offered similar road manners but were considerably more expensive, both to buy and to run.

The 99mph Capri 1600GT, for example, was priced at just £1,041 in February 1969,

Did You Know?

Ford never offered an open-air version of the Capri but British specialists Crayford and Abbott did. Crayford's was the more successful of the pair, with about thirty 1600GTs and 2000GTs undergoing conversion at its Westerham workshops in Kent between 1971 and 1972. Massive extra strengthening was needed in the bodyshell once the metal roof had been sliced off.

▼ Kent-based engineering firm Crayford produced this neat Capri soft-top, called it the Caprice, and produced about thirty conversions.

Here's an example of the Capri built for the North American market, where it was astonishingly successful with some half-a-million sold.

while the MGB GT cost £21 more. Although it was marginally faster, the MG was still no more than a cramped two-seater with room in the back for two toddlers. The Sunbeam Rapier H120 offered much the same accommodation as the Capri, but at £1,323 was significantly more expensive, and only about 2mph faster despite its tuned 1725cc engine. The Scimitar GTE came close to matching the performance and accommodation of the Capri in £1,400 3000GT form. In fact, it used the same

◄ A handful of experimental Capris were equipped with four-wheel drive; this superb example is owned by Ford today and is in spectacular working order.

Did You Know?
Ford Motorsport at Boreham in Essex built a handful of MkI 3000GTs equipped with Ferguson Formula four-wheel drive. Roger and Stan Clark amazed TV viewers by driving these high-grip cars in the 1969 winter Rallycross series.

128bhp V6 engine and so, strangely, pre-dated this first truly high-performance Capri by several months. But the Reliant's £1,759 price and specialised nature put it beyond the vital mass-market appeal of the £1,291 Ford.

Motor magazine, in the space of one year, subjected the MkI Capri to its road test scrutiny in 1300GT, 2000GT and 3000GT forms. Assessing the two smaller-engined cars side by side, the mag said: '[They] surprised us by their astonishing quietness

FACTS & DATA: CAPRI MKI 3000GT

Announced: 1969

Engine capacity, configuration: 2994cc, V6

Engine bore/stroke: 93.66/72.44mm

Engine power output: 128bhp @ 4750rpm

Fuel system: single twin-choke carburettor

Bodystyle: two-door, four-seater coupé

Wheelbase: 2559mm

Length: 4262mm

Width: 1646mm

Height: 1275mm

Top speed: 114mph

Acceleration, 0–60mph: 9.2 seconds

Fuel consumption, average: 20mpg approx

Price when new: £1,291 (in 1969)

▲ Rallycross Capris lit up Saturday afternoon TV sport in the 1970s, such as this one expertly handled by the great Roger Clark.

and refinement, and by the excellence in both cars of the gearchange, as well as the clutch and throttle action. In all these departments, this brace of Fords put to shame a so-called "thoroughbred" Italian car that we had on test at the same time.' They said the 1300GT 'performs creditably for its size', at the same time as noting that,

The 3000E was the ultimate luxury version of the Capri at the start, here showing off its very fetching vinyl roof.

➤ Top 1970s getaways: a tasty Capri, a package holiday in the sun by jet or, preferably, a trip to the airport in one to catch the other.

➤➤ A naked Capri lolling on a bed for your delectation, in what has to be the most bizarre car publicity shot of all time.

because it weighed 2cwt more than an Escort 1300, it would inevitably feel 'a little sluggish'. The 2-litre car was, obviously, much more responsive and faster in all instances, and yet fuel economy was little different between the two of them – 26mpg overall in the 1300, and 23 in the 2000.

The 3000GT was rated as having 'an impressive performance in every way' and they loved the entertaining, rear-drive handling – 'excellent balance and practically no roll'. But they bemoaned the lack of overdrive for the four-speed gearbox, feeling this would turn it into a proper, trans-continental cruiser.

Throughout the early 1970s, the Capri reigned supreme in its newly established market sector. It combined affordable style, a satisfying driving experience, and decent build-quality. The long bonnet made any Capri look like it had a powerful V8 engine under there, although the typical car had

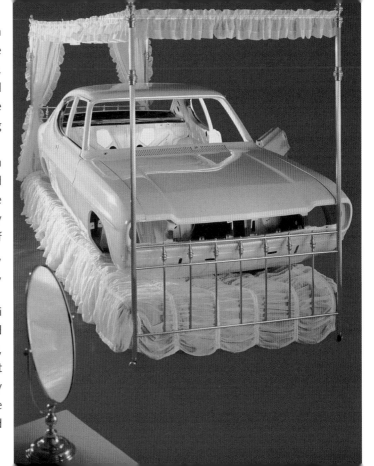

a 2.0-litre V4 like that in the Corsair. The knife-like swage line and dummy brake-cooling ducts down each flank were styling genius.

Its simple but effective Escort-derived suspension – McPherson struts at the front, and a tightly-tethered leaf-sprung 'live' rear axle – made for good, predictable handling, reliable disc/drum brakes did their job well and the four-speed manual transmissions offered a crisp, tactile gearchange. All Capris (with the possible exception of the 84mph standard 1300) were great to drive, and you could just about coax the ton out of a 1600 on a long, straight, downhill stretch of road.

And yet inside every Capri was the unexpected bonus of four genuinely full-size 'bucket' seats.

Did You Know?

Ford Germany developed their own V6-engined RS2600 as a 'homologation special' – a limited-run road/race car to qualify for the European Touring Car Championship after they somehow convinced the sport's governing body, the FIA, it was a four-seater saloon car (well, if BMW could do it with the 3.OCSi, why not Ford with the Capri?). It then proceeded to dominate the Championship in 1971 and 1972.

◀ The Capri RS2600 was a fiery German-built special designed for racing, with alloy wheels and half-bumpers as standard.

ealers couldn't keep up with demand, shifting 213,979 in '69, and in 1970 annual Capri sales reached their all-time peak of an incredible 238,913. That meant Capris accounted for one in every four cars Ford of Europe made, and sales outstripped the company's expectations by 100 per cent. After being so intensely trendy, it was little surprise that yearly sales waned somewhat in 1971 to 209,839, although by 1973, orders had rebounded to 233,325. Ford rarely allowed itself to rest on its laurels, and the Capri came in for improvements almost constantly. The first came as early as September 1970, when every car in the range was given power-assisted brakes as standard issue, as well as much more effective lighting. By the year-end, available option packs had been narrowed down to L, XL and XLR. The 1300GT model was axed but the 3000GT/E got a lusty power hike to 138bhp, achieved with a hotter camshaft, larger inlet valves, reshaped inlet ports and larger jets in the twin-choke carburettor; plus tubular exhaust manifolds, a 3.09:1 final drive and new gearbox ratios.

The most thorough revamp of the range, though, came in September 1972, when no fewer than 151 specification changes were announced. The major ones included larger rear light clusters, a revised fascia, and

Did You Know?

The company organised one-model MkI Capri celebrity races in which characters like Colin Chapman and Frank Williams behaved like banger race drivers, and few of the factory-provided fleet of cars emerged without dents.

redesigned seats that gave more legroom for rear-seat passengers. A notable change under the bonnet was the replacement of the 1600 crossflow by the overhead-camshaft Pinto unit of the same capacity. Automatic transmission was a newly added option, and the suspension was worked over to give a more comfortable ride and

◄ Capri MkI celebrity races resulted in some exciting moments that pleased the crowds and put plenty of dents into the Ford-supplied cars.

better wheel control, partly thanks to a rear anti-roll bar. Close scrutiny of the new Capri brochure would reveal that the 3000E had gone, replaced by a 3000GXL version with four round headlamps instead of two oblong ones.

What about the opposition? Well, it really was caught napping. Opel had been

▶ This German-campaigned three-car Ford Capri team took part in the 1972 Le Mans 24-hour race, seen here in the pits during practice.

◄ MkI Capris were formidable competitors in British and European Touring car races, where they qualified as four-seater saloons.

first out of the starting gate. It surely must have got wind of the Capri's development and quickly created the Manta on the basis of the Ascona saloon, both cars arriving in 1970. It would always be quite rare in Britain. In fact, more commonly encountered was Toyota's Capri-rivalling Celica, also of 1970, a good-looking four-seater GT with a spirited performance, but at a time when Japanese cars were still looked down upon

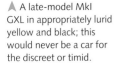

▲ A late-model MkI GXL in appropriately lurid yellow and black; this would never be a car for the discreet or timid.

by many Britons. Vauxhall's answer to the Capri, the Viva/Firenza/Magnum coupé, was never more than an also-ran – as was the Renault 15/17. The Fiat 124 Coupé was a fine-handling, handsome machine but getting long in the tooth and, well, carrying a reputation for fragility on Britain's

unforgiving, and regularly salted, roads. The rotary-engined Mazda RX3 was just plain weird.

Yet Ford was extremely anxious not to let its carefully planned success story fizzle out. As the millionth Capri was built in August 1973, the finishing touches were being put to its replacement, and in December the old one was ousted from the production lines by the Capri II, which was duly unveiled in February 1974 once plentiful supplies were at Ford dealers.

The Capri II presented a masterful reworking of a still attractive basic concept. It was slightly longer and wider, with a style that had been softened, modernised and cleaned up, losing the hockey-stick swage line and dummy air intakes but keeping the distinctive side window line. However, the biggest surprise was that the car now came with a big, hatchback-style tailgate and individually folding rear seat backs that, together, transformed the car's previously mediocre versatility. It was now something of a sporting estate car, like the Reliant Scimitar. True, the tailgate didn't open down to bumper level, so getting a heavy case over the threshold was something of a struggle, but another benefit was that, thanks to enlarged side windows, the cabin was more airy – and slightly roomier.

Immediately obvious was the smaller steering wheel that gave a more civilised driving position, while MkI owners would have been interested to see that the dashboard was carried over entirely from the old car, so the environment was reassuringly

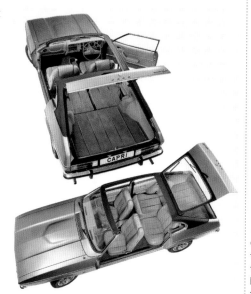

◄ A major feature of the Capri II was its hatchback tailgate but the split folding rear seats also broke new design ground for a sporty coupé.

69

70

Did You Know?

Ford recognised the psychological importance of a bulging bonnet when it revised the Capri in June 1972; from that point on, all cars came with the more muscular-shaped engine cover that had previously been reserved solely for the hairy 3000s.

familiar. In fact, had you been able to see the Capri without its neat new clothes on, you'd have seen the old car underneath pretty much intact because the floorpan, front bulkhead and engine-bay metal was all virtually the same. You'd also have noticed the added strengthening parts needed for the hatchback, and the extra soundproofing materials, which made the Capri II a heavier car than its illustrious predecessor.

FACTS & DATA: CAPRI MKII 2000

Announced: 1974
Engine capacity, configuration: 1993cc, straight-four cylinder
Engine bore/stroke: 90.8/76.9mm
Engine power output: 98bhp @ 5200rpm
Fuel system: single twin-choke carburettor
Bodystyle: two-door, four-seater coupé
Wheelbase: 2559mm
Length: 4288mm
Width: 1698mm
Height: 1298mm
Top speed: 108mph
Acceleration, 0–60mph: 11.1 seconds
Fuel consumption, average: 26mpg approx
Price when new: £1,687 (in 1974)

So much for the fabric of the basic car – how about the Capri's famously wide choice of options? The complex menu-pricing system of 'packs' was ditched, and the initial range consisted of six fixed-specification

◀ Much of the Capri II's hidden architecture was carried over from the original car, although because of the new third door and its frame it would be rather heavier.

◄◄ The distinctive side window shape was retained for the MkII, although the bodyside hockey stick swage line of its predecessor was dispensed with.

◄ A Capri II 2000GT showing how useful it could be for outdoor types; a contrasting vinyl roof was once again a popular option.

models from the start. At the bottom was the 1300L that retained the trusty yet mild 1298cc Kent overhead-valve motor; then came the 1600L, 1600XL and 1600GT using the 1593cc Pinto unit, and also the 2000GT with a 1993cc Pinto engine that finally confined the little-liked and rather coarse 2-litre V4 to history. At the top of the pile was the 116mph 3000GT with the 2994cc Essex V6 under its swoopy-looking bonnet.

▶ The commodious MkII boot space is shown by this Capri Ghia. Still, that's quite a high sill to hoick a heavy suitcase over . . .

▶▶ The Capri II was the second of Ford's European cars to get the opulent Ghia livery, milking the Italian coachbuilding name for all it was worth.

Did You Know?

It proved tricky to repeat the impact of the first Capri. When, in 1972, Henry Ford II viewed a prototype for a Capri replacement without the car's distinctively rounded rear quarter-window, he apparently barked: 'This ain't Capri!' and demanded a redesign.

1976 Mk2 Ford Capri
Best Mk2 Capri 2009

TBU 474R

There are just over 9,000 Capris left in Britain, and here's one of the finest survivors, an absolute peach of a MkII 3.0 Ghia.

Ford's dominance of the British car market was built on supplying fleets, such as this consignment of Capri IIs for an adventurous car leasing company.

Most cars could be ordered with Ford's own C3 automatic gearbox and power-assisted steering.

But within weeks, there were some new Capri variations. Ford had acquired Italy's Ghia design studio in 1973, and now

➤ A chance here to admire the alloy wheels and the opening rear quarterlights on this Capri II 3.0-litre.

started branding its cars with that historic name and its shield-shaped crest, beginning with the Granada and moving next to the Capri in spring 1974. Available in 2- and 3-litre form, the Ghia package included alloy wheels, tinted glass, a tilt-or-slide sunroof, and special bodyside mouldings. It had about as much to do with Italian coachbuilding tradition as Pizza Hut's deep pan offerings represent pizza made at home by Italian mammas, but the car-buying public was entranced nonetheless.

The bald sales figures appear to show that the new car was a flop, as sales were just 100,000 in 1975. However, a huge part of this massive decline is accounted for by the fact that the Capri II was not initially sold in the USA, where the MkI perhaps surprisingly had accounted for tens of thousands of sales each year. Other factors also gnawed away at the Capri's formerly untouchable market performance. The major one was

the global economy, which in 1974 was in the doldrums because of a 70 per cent jump in oil prices after Egypt and Syria jointly invaded Israeli territory and sparked a bitter conflict. A savage recession ensued,

Did You Know?

Just a few weeks before the Capri MkII was revealed, the special RS3100 went on sale – a 3000GT with an overbored 3.1-litre engine, 148bhp of power and a huge rear ducktail spoiler and front airdam. A thousand of them were to be made at Halewood (although, in the end, it was only 248) to homologate it as a production racer. It cost £2,450, £800 more than a 3000E. Special versions with 3.4-litre Cosworth-modified engines pumping out 455bhp won four major European touring car races.

➤ X-Pack body kits, including fat wheelarches and a front spoiler, could be fitted by your dealer to a 3.0S, as here, to accommodate extra-wide wheels.

Even the standard Capri II could provide some on-track entertainment, as here where car-mad DJ Noel Edmonds piles the pressure on to an Alfa Romeo Alfetta in a standard production car race.

and by December '73 Britain was enduring a three-day working week, frequent power cuts, and a 10.30 p.m. curfew on its three TV channels. New cars were far from most people's minds, particularly ones that even hinted at fun and frivolity.

But the Capri II, with its old-fashioned drivetrain and resolute lack of high-tech equipment, was perhaps even then seeming a little creaky. The world was moving on. The Volkswagen Scirocco, a fellow 1974 debutante, was a swift and

➤ Even in plain, unadorned and basic form, a Capri II was a tasty-looking motor, especially in bright yellow.

stylish alternative with more surefooted if less unruly front-wheel drive, and a year later VW would ignite the 'hot hatchback' craze with its compact, fuel-injected Golf GTI. If it had to be a sensible, family-friendly GT then almost every Japanese importer had something of reasonable calibre to offer, and if you had the dosh then there was the considerable added cachet of owning a new small Porsche, the 924.

Rather than change tack, Ford decided to fight back with an ongoing programme of enhancements and promotions to keep the Capri II uppermost in enthusiasts' minds. On the race tracks of Europe, in rounds of the European Touring Car Championship, 3-litre Capris were continuing to put up great performances, regularly walloping the predominant BMWs. To capitalise on this, Ford sprang a surprise at the Geneva Motor Show on 1 March 1975.

Did You Know?

The only Capri with a V8 engine was the Perana V8, a clever transplant carried out from 1970 in South Africa by Basil Green Motors, with approval from Ford. A tuned 5-litre Ford Fairlane engine and Mustang four-speed gearbox was fitted into an otherwise standard Capri 3000XL, the resulting hot rod accelerating from standstill to 60mph in 6.1 seconds, helped by a limited-slip differential. The lowered car was only 9kg heavier yet had a 142mph top whack. Several hundred of these surprisingly refined cars were built, and many were successfully raced.

◄◄ US-specification Capri II: the short-lived car was axed after Ford decided to launch a rebadged version of its Mustang III, the Mercury Capri, to take its place.

◄ In 1976 Ford offered an 'economy' 1.3-litre Capri II in the midst of a fuel crisis, with basic trim and cheap, black-painted bumpers.

The limited edition model was called the 'Midnight Special', and was resplendent in its lustrous black paintwork with extensive gold pinstripe coachlining reminiscent of the John Player Lotus F1 livery of the period. The all-black interior had gold cloth inserts to the seats, and the car sat on special, fat gold alloy wheels. Subtle it was not. But it was a nifty mover, thanks to stiffer suspension and shock absorber settings that sharpened up the driving experience substantially over the generally rather spongy mainstream Capris. Engine choice was 1.6-, 2- or 3-litre.

A toned-down standard version of this firmer-handling Capri joined the permanent range in October 1975, and it would be the final significant change to the Capri II line-up, as Ford shifted its close attention to launching the Fiesta and new versions of the Escort, Cortina and Granada.

Did You Know?
The most popular engine size across the whole spectrum of Capris was the 1.6, which – at 550,000 – accounted for more than a quarter of all versions sold.

◀ This eye-catching Midnight Special copied the black-and-gold livery of the race-winning Lotus JPS Formula 1 team, and previewed the regular production Capri S.

In March 1978 there arrived a new Capri, the Capri MkIII. For anyone impressed by Ford's bold move to front-wheel drive with the attractive little Fiesta, it would be a disappointment. Here was a comprehensive revamp rather than another radical new model. Yet for the sporty coupé's established fanbase, it was a case of the best just getting better, and fie to the increasingly high-tech car world charging ahead around their beloved.

Engineers, Ford claimed, had incorporated 150 revisions to mechanical and structural components, which may well

> Spring 1978 and the new Capri MkIII arrives, here gracing the cover of Ford's monthly updated all-models brochure.

Did You Know?

Many cars are developed under codenames to keep them secret from rivals and the media. The title of the Capri MkII project before it was made public was 'Diana'; the MkIII was 'Carla'.

◄ The Capri III's refined aerodynamics are clearly shown on this 2.0 GL with its front airdam and carefully shaped grille vanes.

have been true, but most of them were tiny adjustments, and most of those were concerned with the new bonnet, grille and front chin spoiler. That said, the Capri III's revised visage was the result of close attention to improve aerodynamics, with a grille whose aerofoil slats did an extremely good job at cutting drag at sustained high speeds, and a streamlined front valance. S models gained a neat black rubber rear spoiler too. The results were so good, in fact, that the 3.0S version's top speed rose

and now extending right round to the wheelarches. Laminated windscreens were standard-fit across the board, and Ford claimed that running costs were slashed by 44 per cent over two years after it decreed major service intervals could be extended to 12,000 miles.

Otherwise, the range nomenclature was largely as before: 1300L or GL; 1600L, GL or S; 2.0 GL, S or Ghia; and 3.0S or Ghia. In Germany, the line-up was the same except that 2.0- and 2.3-litre V6 engines were also offered, in S and Ghia editions.

As it turned out, there was very little need for Ford to promote the Capri III. The car got plenty of attention, and TV air time, as one of the regulars of *The Professionals*. Britain's answer to *Starsky & Hutch* was must-see Saturday night viewing from 1977 to 1983 for its tough and action-packed portrayal of the fictional 'Criminal Intelligence 5' government agency, overseen by George

by 8mph to 122mph, with a full second shaved from its 0–60mph time to 8.5 seconds.

All Capris now enjoyed four circular headlamps peeking out from under the 'eyebrow' of the lowered bonnet's leading edge for a mean-looking stance. The bumpers were new, too, all matt-black

all built its mystique over the years. Viewed today, its misdemeanours seem mild – the main characters may not be politically correct but there's pretty tame swearing,

◄ The squat, purposeful stance of the Capri III 3.0S – just the kind of car that delighted TV audiences in the hands of *The Professionals*.

Cowley (played, with dourness and ferocity, by Gordon Jackson), and his two finest operatives – William Bodie (Lewis Collins), a former SAS tough nut, and Doyle (Martin Shaw), an ex-copper.

Their special status meant fast cars were genuine tools of their trade, and they were driven to near-destruction in the pursuit – literally – of everyone from terrorists to racial supremacists. *The Professionals* was condemned at the time for its violence, laddishness and lairy driving, which have

FACTS & DATA: CAPRI MKIII 1600

Announced: 1978

Engine capacity, configuration: 1593cc, straight-four cylinder

Engine bore/stroke: 87.67/66mm

Engine power output: 72bhp @ 5500rpm

Fuel system: single carburettor

Bodystyle: two-door, four-seater coupé

Wheelbase: 2563mm

Length: 4376mm

Width: 1698mm

Height: 1323mm

Top speed: 98mph

Acceleration, 0–60mph: 13.5 seconds

Fuel consumption, average: 35mpg

Price when new: £3,101 (in 1978)

▶ Bumpers that wrapped around to the wheelarches and chunky side rubbing strips gave a major visual update to the Capri III, here in 3.0 Ghia form.

Did You Know?

One notable film appearance for the Capri MkII was in the 1975 movie *Brannigan*. It features prominently in a car chase through South London that culminates with it jumping the widening gap between the rising bascules of Tower Bridge. At the wheel through some of this action is the film's star . . . John Wayne!

precious little gore, and several stories that touch raw nerves and should, therefore, have been applauded. The Bodie/Doyle banter is fairly entertaining and the action, often filmed on London's streets, seems impossibly realistic by today's anodyne standards.

◄ This shot of a 1979 3.0 Ghia shows how Ford's use of matt black painted metal had changed from austerity measure to style enhancer.

At first, a tie-up with British Leyland saw cars like the Princess, Rover SD1, Triumph TR7 and Triumph Dolomite in the show but the producers soon switched to Ford, which gladly supplied cars for filming. A Capri, a highly unusual X-pack MkII 3000GT in silver, had appeared briefly in the first series in Doyle's hands, while Bodie had enjoyed a

bronze 3.0-litre Ghia; for series two (1978), however, Bodie had a silver MkIII 3.0S, and two identical cars were used for filming.

Doyle was issued with a white Ford Escort RS2000 that he used in 1978 and 1979 episodes. Both men used a variety of gold and silver Capri 3.0Ss in 1980 and 1981. 'We definitely wanted to "bulk up" the imagery of the characters,' creator Brian Clemens recalled of the hard-driven, wheel-spinning Capris that undoubtedly imbued Bodie and Doyle (albeit often portrayed by stunt drivers) with more on-screen grit. The association kept the Capri uppermost in the mind of every wannabe boy racer, despite the car's advancing years. And although the many Fords used in *The Professionals* were returned to the manufacturer and then became everyday used cars, almost all of them are now owned by fans of the series, and most are in fine fettle.

Producers of ITV's *Minder* also did their bit to give the Capri some macho, early '80s cred; Terry McCann (Dennis Waterman) was often shown to be a Capri driver on his

◁ Once again, dealer-fitted X-Pack parts like flared glassfibre wings and extra-wide wheels were on offer to turn a Capri III into a 'café racer'.

◁ By 1981, when this brochure was issued, the Escort XR3 was Ford's fast car focus, yet the trusty Capri was still promoted as a lifestyle-enhancing choice.

⬆ Bold plaid upholstery patterns were a notable feature in early 1980s Capris, stitched on to body-hugging Recaro sports seats in the case of the S models.

various errands and scrapes looking after roguish car dealer Arthur Daley (George Cole).

Nevertheless, by 1980 Capri sales had fallen to an annual total of 41,755, and even Ford itself was apparently retreating from the sporty coupé arena and moving into trendy 'hot hatchbacks' with the 1981 launch of the Escort XR3. By 1982 UK Capri sales dipped below 26,000.

There was one way to keep interest simmering, and that was to issue the Capri in regular limited editions. The first, in 1980, was the 1600L-based GT 4,

German team Zakspeed ran Capris in 1970s Group 5 DRM racing championships, adding major aerodynamic enhancements, shown here being evaluated in model form, to the cars to get results.

whose title paid homage to the wildly modified cars of the Zakspeed Capri racing team. Wild, though, the GT4 was not, offering little more than a few additional instruments with red highlights, and some stripes on the side and bonnet. Alongside it was the Capri Calypso, with a two-tone paintjob.

◀◀◀ Zakspeed Capri driver Klaus Ludwig won the overall DRM championship in 1981; here he is at speed at Germany's Nürburgring circuit.

◀ It's 1979 at the Zolder circuit in Austria, and the winning Zakspeed Capri is seen in its usual position – that of holding off furious competition from BMWs.

Did You Know?

It was so easy to convert a MkII into a MkIII that Ford Motorsport issued conversion kits – front-end/bonnet panels, headlamps, and a spoiler – so racing customers could upgrade the looks of their Capris without replacing them.

▲ Ford tried to cash in on the Zakspeed racing success with this GT-4 limited edition, although the special treatment extended only to fancy insignia.

Then came the 1.3 or 1.6 Cameo and Tempo of 1981, bargain-basement machines shorn of bits and pieces to bring them in at a very tempting £3,995. The Cabaret, Cabaret II and Calypso II continued the short-run duotone theme throughout 1982.

However, while all this small-time tinkering was being organised by Ford's marketing team, the high-performance Capri was being readied for a mighty comeback. The result was first seen at the Geneva Motor Show in March 1981: the 2.8 Injection.

It was a remarkable transformation of the old warhorse, undertaken by Ford's newly established Special Vehicle Engineering at Dunton, Essex, under the supervision of leading company department engineer Rod Mansfield. In place of the old 'Essex' 3-litre V6 was the 'Cologne' 2.8-litre V6, a much more modern design as used in the most upmarket Ford Granada. To this was added Bosch K-Jetronic fuel injection to produce a 160bhp unit. The car's chassis had then been comprehensively uprated to handle the potent new power unit. Lowered suspension was tuned and stiffened with thicker anti-roll bars and gas-filled shock absorbers, and the car rode on wide-rim

◀ Only 200 of these Capri 2.8 Turbos were built, using a single KKK turbocharger attached to a carburettor Granada 2.8-litre V6 engine.

➤ The Capri range for Britain taken from a Ford brochure in about 1981, although much reduced, still endeavoured to offer an attractive sporty package for all types of driver.

Did You Know?

In 1981, Ford had around 200 cars converted to so-called Capri Turbo specification by the German tuning company behind the highly successful Zakspeed race team. They all had 2.8-litre, carburettor-fed Ford Granada engines and a single KKK turbocharger.

Wolfrace 'pepperpot' alloy wheels fitted with Goodyear's 205/60VR NCT tyres. Front disc brakes were now ventilated. The centrepieces of the smartly trimmed interior were two bodyhugging Recaro sports seats.

It was good looking, reliable, powerful, well equipped and easy to drive fast, perhaps with a touch of satisfyingly controllable oversteer where circumstances allowed. When it finally went on sale

The Ford Capri

in the UK in summer 1982, the critics loved it. 'A car that goes with wonderful eagerness', cooed *Autocar*, fresh from its experience of establishing that the 2.8 Injection could make the 0–60mph sprint in just 7.9 seconds.

'You always know exactly what's happening to the front wheels, which

makes mid-corner steering corrections easy to apply', declared *Motor* as part of its eulogy to the car's taut and enjoyable handling characteristics. It also rated the seats as 'truly superb' and the power-assisted steering as 'quick and precise yet well weighted'.

▲ The Cabaret, resplendent in its natty two-tone paintjob, was one of several special editions designed to keep luring Capri customers into Ford showrooms.

◄◄ As launched in 1982, the Ford Capri 2.8 Injection; this one has the optional two-tone paint finish but the standard 'pepperpot' alloy wheels.

◄ Fuel injection and a modern V6 engine gave the Capri a new and energetic lease of life, transforming it into a 130mph slingshot.

Indeed, the 2.8 Injection's performance – with a 130mph top speed – would make it a match for the Porsche 911SC. What finesse and breeding it ultimately lacked was made up for by the Capri's £7,995 price tag, versus £16,732 for the Porsche. The Capri rendered both the temperamental £10,250 Alfa Romeo GTV6 and the portly £8,641 Datsun 280ZX irrelevant also-rans. The sporty Ford had gained a genuinely new lease of life.

➤ The standard Capri was getting pretty soggy by hot hatchback standards in 1982, but the 2.8 Injection featured carefully stiffened suspension that made it predictable, and great fun, to loon around in.

The rather feeble 1300 models were abandoned in 1982. The following year, in January, the 2.8 Injection received the very worthwhile benefit of a five-speed gearbox, which essentially gave it an identical mechanical package to the Ford Sierra XR4i. In addition, there was upgraded trim in the cabin, a refinement

◄ By June 1984, every Capri model came with a five-speed gearbox . . . and carpet fit that left a lot to be desired in the neatness department!

Did You Know?

The 2.8i S had one of the shortest options lists of any Ford ever offered. The only extra-cost things on it were a choice of metallic or two-tone paintwork.

that spread to the smaller-engined cars in February 1983, which now consisted of the LS and S in 1600 and 2.0 forms; S models simultaneously received the 2.8's sporty suspension tweaks.

It seemed improbable that one of the stars of the 1983 Motorfair motor show at London's Earl's Court would be a Ford Capri, but the prototype Tickford Turbo Capri was an absolute crowd-stopper.

The germ of the idea to turn the 2.8 Injection into a junior Aston Martin Vantage came from ex-Lotus F1 driver and latterly car journalist John Miles. He was convinced that the car was potentially a 140mph machine whose handling could be tuned to match, yet its interior could still be made opulent and cocooned, and he shared his vision with Victor Gauntlett and Bob Lutz, chairmen of Aston Martin and Ford of Europe respectively. Aston's new Tickford division was well-placed to build the car in its Coventry factory, alongside the Jaguar XJ-S Cabriolet, but when Lutz was posted back to the USA by his Ford employers, the venture stalled. Undeterred, Miles and Gauntlett decided to sell the car themselves, with Ford's cautious agreement to supply 250 2.8 Injections on which the Aston Martin stardust would be sprinkled.

The engine was turbocharged to produce 200bhp, there was a limited-slip differential in the transmission to aid grip under hard acceleration, and the reworked so-called A-frame rear suspension was configured to allow rear disc brakes. An impressive looking

Did You Know?

The last British-built Capri was completed in October 1976 at Halewood on Merseyside. Henceforth, all cars were made in Germany, and ironically after 1984 they were destined almost solely for export to the UK. The Halewood plant today is the home of the Land Rover Freelander 2 and Range Rover Evoque.

opulent walnut fillets, electric windows, a sunroof, burglar alarm, and a redesigned centre console trimmed in leather.

It was on sale in November 1983, available in white, red or black, at the slightly outrageous price of £14,985, perhaps indicating that it could have been done for less had it been sold officially through Ford dealers. Indeed, you could spend much more on one by going for a bodykit was designed by Simon Saunders – later the creator of the Ariel Atom fun car – and included side skirts, a deep front airdam, a blanked-out grille (aping the Aston V8 Vantage), and a gigantic rear spoiler. The additions reduced the drag coefficient from 0.39 to 0.37, and Tickford calculated that its modifications reduced front-end lift by 70 per cent. Inside were

◀ In 1984, everyone was talking about Ferrari's Testarossa, so one enterprising accessory company issued these Testarossa-style false air intake stickers especially for Capris – nice.

▼ With inspiration from racing driver John Miles, Tickford turned the Capri 2.8 Injection into a junior Aston Martin Vantage.

full leather interior and Pirelli P7 tyres, and by 1987 the price of the standard car had risen to £17,220! Just 85 examples were, in the end, delivered to fortunate customers. Nonetheless, as *Motor Sport* magazine proved, it was a 'true 140mph supercar'

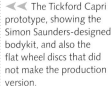

◀◀ The Tickford Capri prototype, showing the Simon Saunders-designed bodykit, and also the flat wheel discs that did not make the production version.

◀ Tickford's interior treatment for the Capri created a cocoon of wood and leather, and added a built-up, leather-covered centre console.

> From 1984, the 2.8 Injection became the 2.8i Special with new RS alloy wheels and a limited-slip differential similar to the Tickford's.

Did You Know?

During the Capri's 18-year lifespan, 1,900,557 examples were built. This breaks down as 1,172,900 MkIs, 403,612 MkIIs, and 324,045 MkIIIs.

that could hurtle from standstill to 60mph in just 6.7 seconds.

In June 1984, all the 1600 and 2.0 cars became Capri Lasers, with a mild cosmetic makeover inside and out, and four-spoke RS alloy wheels, but also with a very welcome five-speed gearbox as standard (still with three-speed automatic optional).

◀ The Ford Sierra XR4i contained, essentially, the exact same mechanical package as the Capri, but in a rather more modern shape.

One of the last few Tickford Capris from 1987, in pearly white paint and with matching 2.8i S wheels.

Every Capri now came with a black spoiler glued to its tailgate.

One spin-off from the 2.8 Injection itself, though, was a Tickford-style limited-slip diff from October 1984 onwards in the subtly renamed 2.8i S. There were new, seven-spoke RS alloy wheels too, along with half-leather trim to match the Recaro seats, and rear seatbelts.

With the Ford Escort XR3i and Sierra RS Cosworth upholding Ford's sports saloon traditions, the good old Capri was now being put out to grass.

◄ Built in Cologne but almost exclusively sold to us Brits, the 280 was a sleek limited edition that would be the Capri's swansong.

Brooklands green was the unique paint finish chosen for the 280, which was extended to the door mirrors on this highly desirable edition.

◀ The 280's leather-upholstered Recaro seats were the ultimate in driver support for the time, and contrasted with the ageing ambience of the rest of the cabin.

Despite its shape dating back thirteen years, and its profile almost two decades old, the Capri 280 remained a rakish-looking car to the end.

Only 27,618 of them were made in 1983 and most of those – some 22,000 – were sold in the UK. In fact, the following year left-hand-drive manufacture stopped altogether, meaning the Capri was now almost exclusively sold in Britain. Sales fell to 9,262 in 1985, and by Christmas 1986, it was finished. However, this was not before a final 'run-out' edition (1,038 of them, to be exact) of a special 2.8 Capri, called the 280, had been built and shipped from Cologne to the UK for sale in early 1987. Its special alloy wheels set off the unique Brooklands green paintwork marvellously.

The Capri had passed on.

The Ford performance spotlight then swung on to such cars as the Sierra RS Cosworth and Escort RS Cosworth. The Capri itself was never replaced, although its name was recycled for a short-lived four-seater convertible produced in Australia between 1989 and '94.

◄ In 1994, Ford attempted to rekindle interest in a four-seater coupé with the US-built, front-wheel drive Probe; its reception from Capri aficionados was chilly, at best.

119

◄◄ Ford's second US export to fill the Capri's hefty boots was the Cougar, briefly on sale from 1998, and another lacklustre offering.

◄ The 1997 Puma was an ingenious little coupé based on the Fiesta. It was cute but, to quote Henry Ford II, 'That ain't Capri.'

> Made in Australia, this neat, Mazda-based open two-seater revived the Capri name between 1991 and '94.

>> In 2011, Ford unveiled this wild Evos concept for yet another new coupé. 'The New Capri!' declared car magazines . . . but is it?

Sold as the Ford Capri down under and the Mercury Capri in the USA, it was based on the front-wheel-drive Mazda 323 and was never even imported to the UK. In 1994, indeed, Ford made a half-hearted attempt to fill the Capri's (platform) shoes in Europe with another sporty, Mazda-based confection – the American-made Ford Probe. It was not much liked, nor very popular, and the same went for the Ford Cougar that replaced it in 1998, despite the edgy lines and the availability of a 2.5-litre Duratec V6 engine. Ford of Europe did a whole lot better with the 1997 Ford Puma but, being based on the Fiesta, it was a rather different kettle of fish.

Visos was the name of this 2003 design
from Ford, a concept car loaded with
classic Capri nuances and details.

Ford's 2005 Iosis concept followed the trend of four-door coupés as a way to resurrect that old Capri magic.

It seems the Capri was a car of its time, and trying to recapture its impact in a different era has been an elusive quest for Ford ever since. One coupé concept car after another – from the Visos in 2003 to the Iosis of 2005 and lately the 2011 Evos – has been revealed yet none has hit the road. And, we must ask ourselves, will one ever? Car fanatics might eulogise the car but, to anyone who didn't grow up in the 1970s, the Capri's slightly ropey image as the wheels of choice for the last-chance-trendy is encapsulated by its regular appearance, beginning in the 1991 episode 'He Ain't Heavy, He's My Uncle', as Derek Trotter's car in the sitcom *Only Fools & Horses*. The car was mercilessly ribbed although, it must be said, Del Boy did get the intonation right: 'The CA-pri Ghia'.

But you never know. One of those car magazines regularly hailing 'The New Capri!' on its front cover might just signal the return of a motoring icon, one day . . .

◄ The good old Capri in its ultimate incarnation, as the 160bhp 2.8 Injection that surprised the motoring world in 1981.

Other titles available in this series

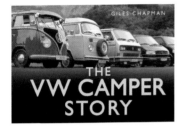

ISBN 978 07524 6281 3

ISBN 978 07524 6282 0

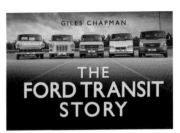

ISBN 978 07524 6283 7

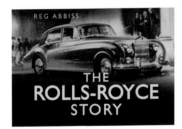

ISBN 978 07524 6614 9

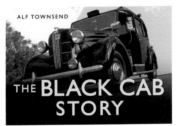

ISBN 978 07509 4853 1

ISBN 978 07524 5084 1